The Chester Books of Madrigals

5. SINGING AND DANCING

Edited by Anthony G. Petti

For Lorna

CHESTER MUSIC

Cover:
May (Taurus/Gemini) from the
Très Riches Heures du Duc de Berry.
Reproduced by kind permission of the Musée Condé, Chantilly.

1. SOL SOL, G G A B C

Sol sol, G G A B C, I come with a love for la sol fa mi re re ut (do) re. Mother, I was going to see someone whom I love very much; and while I was going I sang what I shall now tell you: sol sol, *etc.*

Alonso(early 16th century)

*Approximate pronunciation for English speakers: G= hě, between he(n) and hay; A=ă, between u(p) and ah; B= bě, between be(t) and bay; C= thě (th as in 'thin', ĕ as before).

2. LIEBLICH ICH HÖRTE SINGEN

1. I heard lovely singing as I was crossing over the sea; sirens with their bright voices cheered me: joyful sounds so pleasing to my heart that I would gladly give myself up to such music.
2. But how could I escape it, even if it did gladden my heart? Misfortune would soon bring me great suffering; the sirens and their singing would imperil me and drown me in the sea, where I could not escape death.
3. Dear friend, you must learn who the sirens are: maidens in their prime (so Venus assures us), who with their loveliness pursue many fine young men, and by sugared words beguile their hearts.
4. Their mouths bear honey with which to please, but their hearts are filled with gall to inflict pain. They jeopardize many a man's life, so that he can only despair; therefore he who wants to survive must avoid the love of those maidens.

Johannes Christoph Demantius (1567-1643)

15
ü - ber Meer: 1. Drum solch lieb-lich Ju - bi - lie
freu - et sehr.
getzt mein Herz? 2. Sy - re - nes nach i - rem sin
gross - en Schmerz.
als ich fuhr ü - ber Meer: 1. Drum solch lieb-lich Ju - bi - lie
welchs mich er - freu - et sehr.
welchs mir er - getzt mein Herz? 2. Sy - re - nes nach i - rem sin
bringt mich in gross - en Schmerz.
ich fuhr ü - ber Meer: 1. Drum solch lieb-lich Ju - bi - lie
mich er - freu - et sehr.
mir er - getzt mein Herz? 2. Sy - re - nes nach i - rem sin
mich in gross - en Schmerz.
ü - ber Meer: 1. Drum solch lieb-lich Ju - bi - lie
- freu - et sehr.
- getzt mein Herz? 2. Sy - re - nes nach i - rem sin
gross - en Schmerz.
fuhr ü - ber Meer: 1. Drum solch lieb-lich Ju - bi - lie
er - freu - et sehr.
er - getzt mein Herz? 2. Sy - re - nes nach i - rem sin
in gross - en Schmerz.
mf repeat p
20
1.
2.
- ren mein Herz be-gehrt fern zu hö - ren; - ren; ja,
- gen mich wol-ten in gross gfahr brin - gen, - gen, und
- ren mein Herz be-gehrt fern zu hö - ren; - ren; ja, ich mich wollt er-
- gen mich wol-ten in gross gfahr brin - gen, - gen, und mich ins Meer er-
- ren mein Herz be-gehrt fern zu hö - ren; - ren; ja, ich mich
- gen mich wol-ten in gross gfahr brin - gen, - gen, und mich ins
- ren mein Herz be-gehrt fern zu hö - ren; - ren; ja, ich mich wollt er - ge -
- gen mich wol-ten in gross gfahr brin - gen, - gen, und mich ins Meer er - sauf -
- ren mein Herz be-gehrt fern zu hö - ren; - ren;
- gen mich wol-ten in gross gfahr brin - gen, - gen,
p
Sing, don't steal – photocopying is theft.

3. Gut G'sell ab'r tu erfahren
wer die Syrenen sein:
Jungfraun in brünstign Jahren
(so Venus nimmet ein),
welche manchem frommen Knaben
mit Lieblichkeit tun nachjagen,
und tun mit schönen Reden
sein Herz gänzlich betören.

4. Im Mund sie Hönig haben,
damit sie machen Freud,
Gall ab'r im Herzen tragen,
damit sie schaffen Leid;
tun manchen in Leibs G'fahr jagen,
darinnen er muss verzagen;
drum, wer aus G'fahr will bleiben,
der soll Jungfraun Leib meiden.

3. NUN FANGET AN EIN GUTS LIEDLEIN

Let's begin a nice little song; let the lutes and other instruments play. It is good to make lovely music: therefore play and sing so that everything resounds: help to adorn our festivities.

Hans Leo Hassler(1564-1612)

15
1.
2.
-ment und Lau-ten auch er-klin - gen. -gen. Lieb - lich zu mu-si-zie - ren, will
-ment und Lau-ten auch er-klin - gen. -gen. Lieb-lich zu mu-si - zie-ren, will
-ment und Lau-ten auch er-klin - gen. -gen. Lieb-lich zu mu-si-zie - ren, will
-ment und Lau-ten auch er-klin - gen. -gen. Will
mp
p
20
25
sich jetz - und ge-büh - ren: drum schlagt und singt, dass all's er-klingt, helft
sich jetz - und ge - büh - ren: drum schlagt und singt, dass all's er-klingt, helft un - ser
sich jetz - und ge-büh - ren: drum schlagt und singt, dass all's er-klingt, helft un - ser
sich jetz - und ge-büh - ren: drum schlagt und singt dass all's er-klingt, dass
mf
cresc.
30
un - ser Fest auch zie - - ren, drum schlagt und
Fest, helft un - ser Fest auch zie - ren, drum schlagt und singt, dass
Fest, helft un - ser Fest auch zie - ren, drum schlagt und singt,
all's er - hlingt, helft un - ser Fest auch zie - ren, drum

* *Though clearly intended for STB in the original, the piece is in some ways more effective set for TAB or TTB.*

5. CHANTER JE VEUX

I want to sing of the lovely maiden to whom heaven has revealed all its treasures, all its beauty, and all its precious gifts. She has a noble spirit, excellent sense, and, in short, quite apart from her beauty, she has all that nature ever bestowed on a living creature. Therefore, let us never cease to sing of Catherine in our praise of divine music.

Orlandus Lassus (1532-94)

15
- sors dé - ce - le, Tous les plus beaux et plus ri - ches pré - sents. El -
- ce - le, Tous ses plus beaux et plus ri-ches pré - sents, et plus ri-ches pré -
- sors dé - ce - le, Tous ses plus beaux et plus ri - ches pré - sents, et plus ri-ches pré -
- ce - le, Tous ses plus beaux et plus ri - ches pré - sents.
- le, Tous ses plus beaux et plus ri - ches pré-sents.
mf
15
p
20
- le a l'e-sprit gen-til, el-le a l'e-sprit gen-til. El - le a le sens ras - sis, El-le a bref tout ce que na-tu-re
- sents. El - le a l'e-sprit gen-til, El - le a le sens ras - sis, El-le a bref tout ce que na-tu-re, El-
- sents. El-le a l'e-sprit gen-til, el-le a l'e-sprit gen-til. El - le a le sens ras - sis, El-le a bref tout ce que na-tu-re, El -
El - le a l'e-sprit gen-til, el-le a l'e-sprit gen-til, El-le a le sens ras-sis, El-le a bref tout ce que na-tu-re, El -
El-le a l'e-sprit gen-til, El - le a le sens ras - sis, El -
20
p
mp

25
(joint la beau - té) mit onc en cré - a - tu - re. Ne ces - sons donc, ne ces - sons donc
le a bref tout ce que na - tu - re (joint la beau - té) mit onc en cré - a - tu - re. Ne ces-sons donc, ne ces - sons donc de
le a bref tout ce que na - tu - re (joint la beau - té) mit onc en cré - a - tu - re. Ne ces - sons donc, ne ces - sons donc de
le a bref tout ce que na - tu - re. Ne ces - sons donc, ne ces - sons donc
le a bref tout ce que na - tu - re. Ne ces - sons donc, de
25
mp
mp
mf
mf
p
mf

30
de chan-ter Ca-the-ri - ne, de chan - ter Ca-the-ri - ne, de chan-ter Ca - the-ri - ne
chan-ter Ca-the-ri - ne, de chan-ter Ca - the-ri - ne, de chan - ter Ca - the - ri - ne En ex - al - tant la
chan-ter Ca-the-ri - ne, de chan - ter Ca-the-ri - ne, de chan - ter Ca - the - ri - ne, En ex - al - tant,
de chan-ter Ca - the - ri - ne, de chan-ter Ca-the-ri - ne, de chan-ter Ca - the - ri - ne Ex ex - al -
chan-ter Ca-the - ri - ne, de chan-ter Ca - the - ri - ne, de chan-ter Ca - the - ri - ne En ex - al - tant la
30
mp

35
40
En ex-al - tant,
en ex-al - tant la mu-si -
musique di-vi - ne, en ex - al - tant la mu-si-que di - vi - ne, en ex-al - tant la mu-si-que
en ex-al - tant la mu-si - que di - vi - ne, en ex - al - tant la mu - si -
-tant la musique di - vi - ne, en ex-al-tant, en ex-al-tant la musique di-vi - ne,
mu - si - que di - vi - ne, en ex - al - tant la mu-si - que di - vi - ne,
35
40
mp
mf
mp

45
- que di - vi - ne, la mu-si - que di - vi - ne.
di-vi - ne, en ex - al - tant la mu - si-que di-vi - ne, en ex-al-tant la mu-si-que di-vi - ne.
- que di - vi - ne, en ex-al - tant la mu-si-que di-vi - ne, en ex-al-tant la mu - si - que di-vi - ne.
en ex-al - tant la mu - si - que di-vi - ne.
en ex-al - tant la mu - si - que di-vi - ne, la mu-si - que di - vi - ne.
45
rall.
mf
mp
mp

6. TUTTO LO DÌ

All day long you tell me: sing, sing! Can't you see I've got no breath left? What's the point of all this singing? I wish you'd tell me to ring, not the bell for nones, but your cymbal. O, if I survive, fa la la, I'd like to have you beneath me.

Orlandus Lassus (1532-94)

15
— che tan - to can-ta - re? Vor - ria che mi di - ces - si: so - na, so -
tan - to can - ta - re? Vor - ria che mi di - ces - si: so - na, so -
- to can - ta - re? Vor - ria che mi di-ces - si: so - na, so -
- to can - ta - re? Vor - ria che mi di - ces si: so - na, so -
15
20
- na, so - na, so - na, Non le cam - pan' a no - na, non le cam - pan' a no -
- na, so - na, so - na, Non le cam - pan' a no - na, non le cam - pan' a no -
- na, so - na, so - na, Non le cam - pan' a no - na, non le cam - pan' a no -
- na, so - na, so - na, Non le cam - pan' a no - na, non le cam - pan' a no -
20
25
30
- na, non le cam-pan' a no - na, non le cam-pan' a no - na Ma
- na, non le cam-pan' a no - na, non le cam - pan' a no - na Ma
- na, non le cam-pan' a no - na, non le cam-pan' a no - na Ma
- na, non le cam-pan' a no - na, non le cam - pan' a no - na Ma
25
30

[♩. = 𝅗𝅥]

35

so cim - ba - lo tuo. O se cam - po ri-ro ro - ri-ro - gne, *O se cam -*

so cim - ba - lo tuo. O se cam - po ri-ro ro - ri-ro - gne, *O se cam -*

so cim - ba - lo tuo. O se cam - po ri-ro ro - ri-ro - gne, *O se cam -*

so cim - ba - lo tuo. O se cam - po ri-ro ro - ri-ro - gne, *O se cam -*

♩. = 𝅗𝅥 mf p

𝅗𝅥 [𝅗𝅥 = ♩.]

40

- po ri-ro ro - ri-ro - gne. S'io t'ag - gio, *s'io t'ag - gio.* s'io t'ag-gio sott' a

- po ri-ro ro - ri-ro - gne. S'io t'ag - gio, *s'io t'ag - gio.* s'io t'ag - gio sott' a st'o -

- po ri-ro ro - ri-ro - gne. S'io t'ag - gio, *s'io t'ag - gio.* s'io t'ag - gio sott' a

- po ri-ro ro - ri-ro - gne. S'io t'ag - gio, *s'io t'ag - gio.* s'io t'ag - gio sott' a

𝅗𝅥 = ♩. mp mf p

45

st'o - gne, s'io t'ag - gio, s'io t'ag - gio, s'io t'ag-gio sott' a st'o - gne.

- gne, s'io t'ag - gio sott' a st'o - gne, s'io t'ag - gio sott' a st'o - gne.

st'o - gne, s'io t'ag - gio, s'io t'ag - gio, s'io t'ag - gio sott' a st'o - gne.

st'o - gne, s'io t'ag - gio, s'io t'ag - gio, s'io t'ag - gio sott' a st'o - gne.

mf f f f rall. mf f

7. SING WE AND CHANT IT

Thomas Morley (1557-1602)

15
Now is best lei - sure To take our plea - sure. Fa la
Let spare no trea - sure To live in plea - sure.
Now is best lei - sure To take our plea - sure. Fa la la la la la la
Let spare no trea - sure To live in plea - sure.
Now is best lei - sure To take our plea - sure. Fa la la la,
Let spare no trea - sure To live in plea - sure.
Now is best lei - sure To take our plea - sure. Fa la la la la
Let spare no trea - sure To live in plea - sure.
Now is best lei - sure To take our plea - sure. Fa la la la la la la
Let spare no trea - sure To live in plea - sure.
15
mf

20
1.
2.
la la la la, fa la la la la. la.
la, fa la la la, fa la la la. la.
fa la la la la la la la, fa la la la la. la.
la, fa la la la la la la, fa la la la la. la.
la, fa la la la la la la la la. la.
20

8. VORRIA CHE TU CANTASS'

I want you to sing me a song while I play the viol;
and I want your words to be *fa mi la mi so la.*

Antonio Scandello (1517-80)

Cantus — Sop.

Vor - ria che tu can - tass' u - na can - zo - ne, *vor - ria che tu can -*

Altus — Alto

Vor - ria che tu can - tass' u - na can-zo - ne, *vor - ria che tu can -*

Tenor — Tenor

Vor - ria che tu can - tass' u - na can-zo - ne, *vor - ria che tu can -*

Bassus — Bass

Vor - ria che tu can - tass' u - na can-zo - ne, *vor - ria che tu can -*

Allegro ♩ = c. 120

mf *p*

10
-o - la, e che di-ces - si, e che di-ces - si:
-o - la, e che di-ces - si, e che di-ces -
8 -o - la, e che di - ces - si e che di - ces - si: fa mi
-o - la, e che di-ces - si, e che di-ces - si:
mp
p
mp
fa mi la mi sol la, fa mi, fa mi la mi sol la, fa mi la mi
-si: fa mi la mi sol la, mi sol la, fa mi la mi sol la, fa
8 la mi sol la mi sol la, fa mi la mi sol la. fa mi la mi
fa mi la mi sol la, fa mi la mi sol la, fa mi la mi sol la, mi
15
mf
mp
1.
2.
20
sol la, fa mi la mi sol la, fa mi la mi sol la. la.
mi so la, fa mi la mi sol la, fa mi la mi sol la. e la.
8 sol la, fa mi la mi sol la. fa mi la mi sol la, e che di - la.
sol la, fa mi la mi sol la, fa mi la mi sol la, e la.
2nd time rall
mf

9. ROUNDS FROM RAVENSCROFT

*groat: a coin worth fourpence.

*This round may be sung with a number of different voice groupings, e.g. Bar./T/A (pitch as suggested), T/A/S (starting a 4th higher), A/Mez./S (5th higher), B/Bar./T (5th lower).

+troll the berry: pass round the wine.

CH 55607

10. THE ELVES DANCE

John Bennet (c.1570-c.1614)

to and fro, to and fro O - ver this green - a. All a-bout, in and out,
to and fro, to ___ and to and fro O - ver this green - a. All a-bout, in and out,
to and fro and fro [and fro] O - ver this green - a. All a-bout, in and out,
fro, to and fro and fro and fro O - ver this green - a. All a-bout, in and out,
mp repeat f

10
all a-bout, in and out, all a-bout, in and out O - ver this green - a.
all a-bout, in and out, all a-bout, in and out O - ver this green - a.
all a-bout, in and out, all a-bout, in and out O-ver ___ this green - a.
all a-bout, in and out, all a-bout, in and out O - ver this green - a.
cresc.
2nd time rall.

11. CHI LA GAGLIARDA

(Villanella alla Napolitana)

1. Fair Ladies, whoever wants to learn the galliard should come to us, for we are fine teachers who night and morning never fail to play tan tan tira.
2. Try it a little and call in whoever you like; after you've done ten turns we leap up, who night and morning never fail to play tan tan tira.
3. So, dear Lady, if you want to learn the galliard, you must do it under the master, for night and day we never fail to play tan tan tira.

Baldassare Donato (c. 1520-1603)

[𝅗𝅥 = 𝅗𝅥] 15 [𝅗𝅥 = 𝅗𝅥]

fi - ni, mae - stri fi - ni, mae - stri fi - ni,
-li - mo, che sa - li - mo, che sa - li - mo, Che di se - ra e da ma - ti - ni mai
te bi - so - gna, te bi - so - gna sta - re,

fi - ni, mae - stri fi - ni, mae-stri fi - ni,
-li - mo, che sa - li - mo, che sa - li - mo, Che di se - ra e da ma - ti -
te bi - so - gna, te bi - so-gna sta - re,

fi - ni, mae - stri fi - ni, mae - stri fi - ni,
-li - mo, che sa - li - mo, che sa - li - mo, Che di se - ra e da ma - ti - ni
te bi - so - gna, te bi - so - gna sta - re,

fi - ni, mae - stri fi - ni, mae - stri fi - ni,
-li - mo, che sa - li - mo, che sa - li - mo, Che di se - ra e da ma - ti -
te bi - so - gna te bi - so - gna sta - re,

cresc. e poco accel. 𝅗𝅥 = 𝅗𝅥 15 mp 𝅗𝅥 = 𝅗𝅥 a tempo mp

20 3 • [𝅘𝅥 = 𝅗𝅥]

man-chia - mo, mai man-chia - mo di so-na - re: Tan tan tan tan - ti-ra, tan tan tan

-ni mai man - chia - mo, mai man-chia-mo di so - na - re: Tan tan tan tan - ti-ra, tan tan tan

mai man - chia - mo, mai man-chia-mo di so - na - re: Tan tan tan tan - ti-ra, tan tan tan

-ni mai man - chia - mo, mai man-chia-mo di so - na - re: Tan tan tan tan - ti-ra, tan tan tan

mf 20 𝅘𝅥. = 𝅗𝅥 = c. 66 f

25

tan - ti-ra, ri - ra ri - ra, tan tan tan tan - ti ra, ri - ra ri - ra, tan tan tan tan - ti ra, ri - ra ri - ra.

tan - ti-ra, ri - ra ri - ra, tan tan tan tan - ti ra, ri - ra ri - ra, tan tan tan tan - ti ra, ri - ra ri - ra.

tan - ti-ra, ri - ra ri - ra, tan tan tan tan - ti ra, ri-ra ri - ra, tan tan tan tan - ti ra, ri - ra ri - ra.

tan - ti-ra, ri - ra ri - ra, tan tan tan tan - ti ra, ri-ra ri - ra, tan tan tan tan - ti ra, ri - ra ri - ra.

25 mp f

12. IL BALLERINO (The Dancer)

Sonatemi un balletto

1. Play me a dance: I want to dance with my sweetheart, for I take great pleasure in the dance, to tell you the truth. (*Refrain*) Come on, what are you doing? Start playing!
2. My nymph is ready and wanting to dance with me, and to favour me still clasps me by the hand. (*Refrain*) Come on, what are you doing? Start playing!

*This piece could be sung by TTB or SSA (A taking the Baritone part an octave higher).

13. SAUTER, DANSER

O, to leap, dance, twirl around, drink red and white wine,
and do nothing all day but count one's money in the sun!

Orlandus Lassus (1532-94)

15
— et ver - meil, blanc et ver - meil, Et ne fai-re rien tous les jours, et ne
et ver - meil, blanc et ver - meil, Et ne fai-re rien, Et ne fai - re rien, Et ne
- meil, blanc et ver - meil, Et ne fai-re rien, et ne fai - re rien, Et ne fai-re
- meil, blanc et ver - meil, Et ne fai-re rien, et ne
f
p
cresc.
fai - re rien tous les jours Que com-pter é - cus au so - leil, que com-pter
fai-re rien tous les jours Que com-pter é-cus au so- leil, que
rien tous les jours Que com-pter é - cus au so - leil, que com pter é - cus au so - leil,
fai-re rien tous les jours Que com-pter é - cus au so-leil, que com-pter é - cus au so -
mp
mf
20
é - cus au so-leil, que com-pter é-cus au so-leil, que com-pter é - cus au so - leil, é - cus au so - leil.
com-pter é - cus au so - leil, au so-leil, Que com-pter é - cus au so-leil, que com-pter é-cus au so - leil.
que com-pter é-cus au so-leil, que com-pter é - cus au so - leil.
- leil, que com - pter é - cus au so - leil, que com-pter é - cus au so-leil, que com-pter é - cus au so - leil.
rall.

14. POURQUOI DONC NE FRINGUERONS-NOUS?

Why don't we go cavorting with our young ladies? Why don't we, in spite of those falsely jealous ones who out of great envy accuse me of foolishly cutting a caper inside the bed-curtains in the evening and early morning? Whatever the case, let me and my friend dance for love. Why don't we frolic despite the falsely jealous ones?

Pierre Passereau (fl. 1509-47)

10
fringue-rons-nous en dépit de ces faux jaloux?
Pourquoi donc ne fringue-rons-nous En dépit de ces faux jaloux?
Pourquoi donc ne fringue-rons-nous, En dépit de ces faux jaloux? Ces faux jaloux, par
jeunes dames? Pourquoi donc ne fringue-rons-nous, En dépit de ces faux jaloux? Ces faux jaloux, par grand en-
10
mf
15
20
Ces faux jaloux, par grand envie,
M'ont mis des
Ces faux jaloux, par grand envie, M'ont mis dessus qu'ai fait fo-
grand envie, par grand envie. M'ont mis dessus qu'ai fait fo-
vie, par grand envie. M'ont mis dessus qu'ai fait folie,
15 mf
20 mp
mp
mp
25
sus qu'ai fait folie D'avoir fringué sous les courti-
lie, qu'ai fait folie D'avoir fringué sous les courtines, d'avoir
lie, qu'ai fait folie D'avoir fringué sous les courtines, sous les courtines.
qu'ai fait folie D'avoir fringué sous les courtines, d'avoir fringué sous
25
mp

30
- nes Fût au soir ou de - vant ma - ti - nes, ou de - vant ma - ti -
frin-gué sous les cour - ti - nes, Fût au soir ou de-vant ma - ti - nes, ou de - vant ma - ti -
Fût au soir ou de - vant ma-ti - nes, fût au soir ou de - vant ma -
les cour - ti - nes. Fût au soir ou de - vant ma - ti - nes, ou de-vant ma - ti -
p
mp
35
- nes: Mais quoi qu'en soit, si dan-se-rons-nous, Moi et mon
- nes: Mais quoi qu'en soit si dan-se-rons-nous, mais quoi qu'en soit, si dan - se - rons - nous. si dan-se-rons-nous,
- ti - nes. Mais quoi qu'en soit, si dan-se-rons-nous, si dan-se-rons-nous,
- nes; Mais quoi qu'en soit, si dan-se-rons-nous, si frin-gue - rons - nous, Moi
mp
mf
40
45
a - mi par a - mours, mais quoi qu'en soit, si
Moi-et mon a - mi par a - mours, mais quoi qu'en soit, si dan-se-rons-nous, mais quoi qu'en soit. si dan - se - rons -
Moi et mon a - mi par a - mours, mais quoi qu'en soit, si dan-se-rons-nous,
et mon a - mi par a - mours, mais quoi qu'en soit, si dan-se-rons-nous,
p
mf

50
dan-se-rons-nous moi et mon a - mi par a - mours. Pour-quoi donc ne frin-gue-rons-nous
- nous, si dan-se-rons-nous, moi et mon a - mi par a-mours. Pour- quoi donc ne frin-gue-rons - nous
si frin-gue-rous-nous, moi et mon a - mi par a - mours. Pour-quoi
si frin-gue-rons - nous, moi et mon a - mi par a - mours.
mp
mf
55
En-tre nos jeu-nes da-mes, pour - quoi donc ne frin-gue-rons-nous, en-tre nos jeu-nes da - mes?
En-tre nos jeu-nes da - mes, en - tre nos jeu-nes da - mes, en - tres nos jeu - nes
donc, pour - quoi donc ne frin-gue-rons-nous En-tre nos jeu-nes da-mes, pour- quoi donc ne frin- gue- rons - nous, en- tre nos
Pour-quoi donc ne frin-gue-rons - nous, pour- quoi donc ne frin - gue- rons - nous, En-tre nos jeu-nes
60
Pour - quoi donc ne frin-gue-rons-nous En dé - pit de ces faux ja - loux?
da - mes? Pour - quoi donc ne frin-gue-rons - nous En dé - pit de ces faux ja - loux?
jeu-nes da - mes? Pour-quoi donc ne frin-gue-rons-nous En dé-pit de ces faux ja - loux?
da - mes, en - tres nos jeu - nes da - mes? Pour-quoi donc ne frin-gue-rons-nous, En dé-pit de ces faux ja - loux?
f
rall.

15. THE SATYRS' DANCE

Thomas Ravenscroft (c. 1582-c. 1635)

*Can be sung a minor third lower by SSTB or SATB.

10
15
fla-ming rays And the im-pe-rial crown of bays, Him with, him with, him with shouts and songs we praise, we
fla-ming rays And the im-pe-rial crown of bays, Him with, him with, him with shouts and songs we praise, we
fla-ming rays And the im-pe-rial crown of bays, Him with, him with, him with shouts and songs we praise, we
fla-ming rays And the im-pe-rial crown of bays, Him with, him with, him with shouts and songs we praise, we
mf
C
20
praise: Ho, ho! That in his boun-ty would vouch-safe to grace The hum-ble,
f
ff
mp
mf
25
hum-ble, hum-ble syl-vans and their shag-gy race.
poco a poco cresc.
poco rall.
f

16. A ROUND OF THREE COUNTRY DANCES IN ONE

* *The allocation and sequence of parts are editorial. Equal or mixed voices, with or without accompaniment, can be used in various permutations, but the Bass should begin and continue throughout.*

** *Petticoat: a short coat worn under the doublet or a jacket.*

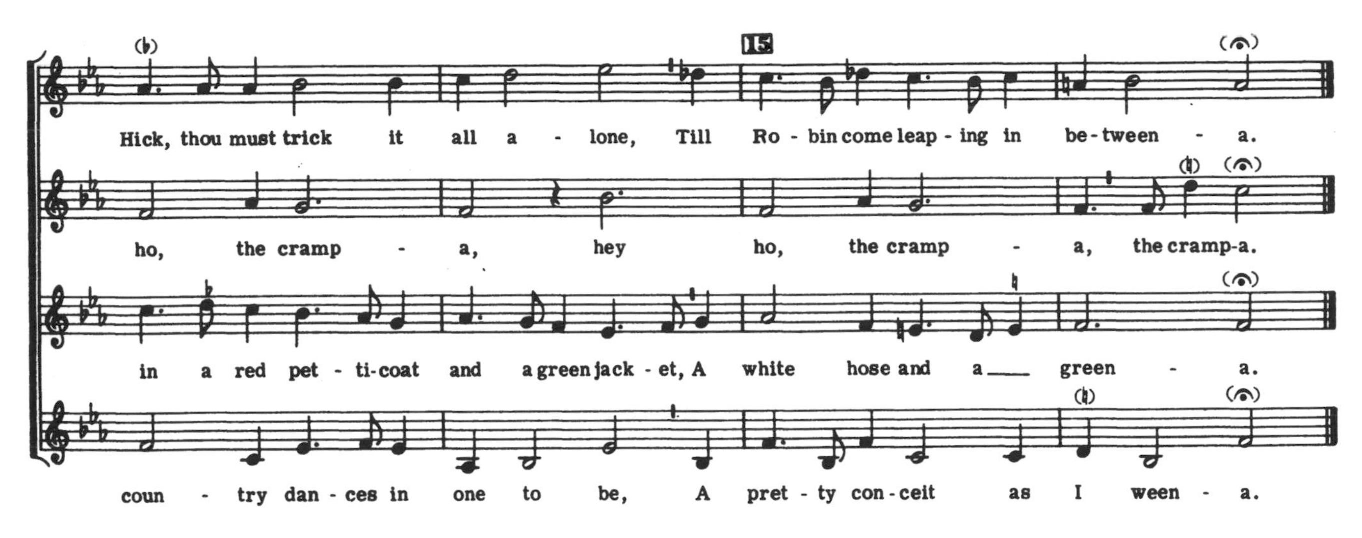

17. STRIKE IT UP, TABOR

Thomas Weelkes (1576-1623)

* *Time change begins bar 8(i) in the original.*

** *Dodkin: a small coin of little value.*

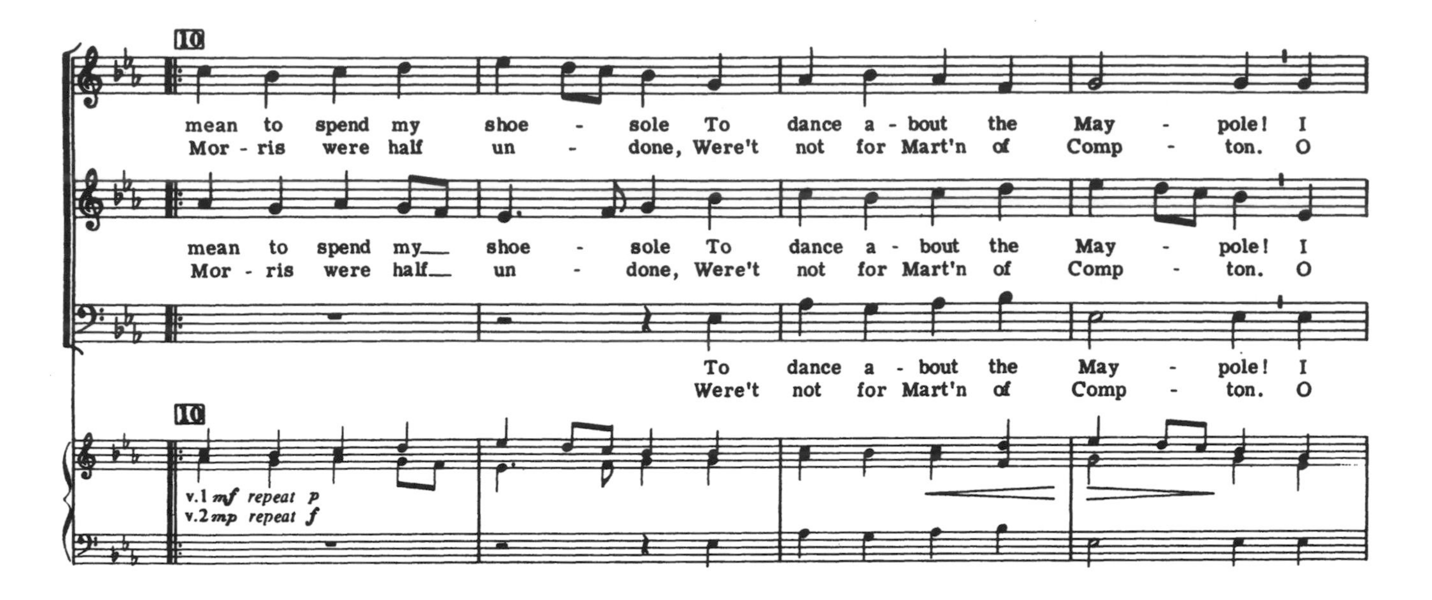
10
mean to spend my shoe - sole To dance a - bout the May - pole! I
Mor - ris were half un - done, Were't not for Mart'n of Comp - ton. O
mean to spend my shoe - sole To dance a - bout the May - pole! I
Mor - ris were half un - done, Were't not for Mart'n of Comp - ton. O
To dance a - bout the May - pole! I
Were't not for Mart'n of Comp - ton. O
10
v.1 mf repeat p
v.2 mp repeat f

15
will be blithe and brisk: Leap and skip, Hop and trip, Turn a - bout In the rout, Un -
well said, jig - ging Al'ce! (♭) Pret-ty Jill, Stand you still! Dap-per Jack Means to smack. How
will be blithe and brisk, blithe and brisk: I'll Leap and skip, Hop and trip, Turn a - bout In the rout, Un -
well said, jig - ging Al'ce, jig - ging Al'ce! [O] Pret-ty Jill, Stand you still! Dap-per Jack Means to smack. How
will be blithe and brisk: Leap and skip, Hop and trip, Turn a - bout In the rout, Un - til
well said, jig - ging Al'ce! Pret-ty Jill, Stand you still! Dap-per Jack Means to smack. How now?
15

20
1. 2.
- til ve - ry wea - ry, wea - ry joints can scarce frisk. I frisk.
now? Fie, fie, fie, fie, fie, fie, fie! you dance false. The false.
- til ve - ry wea - ry, wea - ry joints can scarce frisk. I frisk.
now? Fie, fie, fie, fie, fie, fie, fie! you dance false. The false.
ve - ry wea - ry joints can scarce frisk. frisk.
Fie, fie, fie, fie, fie! you dance false. false.
poco rall. in repeats
20
v.1 dim.
v.2 cresc.
v.1 p
v.2 f

18. TANZEN UND SPRINGEN

1. Dance and leap about, sing and shout, fa la la. Lutes and viols mustn't be silent. Let's make music and enjoy ourselves: that's what I mean to do, fa la la.
2. Pretty maidens in green valleys, fa la la. To go walk with them and chat and have a friendly joke with them cheers my heart much more than silver and gold could.

Hans Leo Hassler(1564-1612)

...Shorter print runs mean higher unit prices...

19. SING WE, DANCE WE

Francis Pilkington (c. 1565-1638)

...Soon the music has to go out of print...

25
30
en - vi - ron - ed, en - vi - ron - ed with all the coun-try swains, Fair-ly trips it o'er the
En-vi - ron - ed with all the coun-try swains, Fair - ly
en-vi - ron - ed, en - vi - ron - ed with all the coun-try swains,
en-vi - ron - ed, with all the coun-try swains, the coun-try
En - vi - ron - ed with all the coun-try swains, coun-try swains,
p
mf
f
pp
35
plains, fair - ly trips it o'er the plains, fair - ly trips it o'er the plains,
trips it o'er the plains, fair - ly trips it o'er the plains,
Fair - ly trips it o'er the plains, fair - ly trips it,
swains, Fair - ly trips it o'er the plains, fair - ly trips it o'er the plains, fair - ly trips it o'er the
Fair - ly trips it o'er the plains, o'er the plains, fair - ly trips it o'er the plains,
mp
mf

40
fair - ly trips it o'er the plains. Let us a -bout, let us a - bout these daf-fa-dil-lies sweet,
fair - ly trips it o'er the plains. Let us a -bout, let us a - bout these daf-fa-dil-lies sweet,
fair - ly trips it o'er the plains. Let us a -bout, let us a - bout these daf-fa-dil-lies sweet, let us a -
plains. fair - ly trips it o'er the plains. Let us a -bout, let us a - bout. let us a-bout these
fair - ly trips it o'er the plains. Let us a -bout, let us a - bout, let us a-bout these
40

45
these daf - fa-dil-lies sweet, these daf - fa - dil - lies sweet
a - bout these daf-fa-dil-lies sweet, a - bout these daf - fa - dil - lies sweet
- bout these daf - fa - dil - lies sweet, these daf - fa - dil - lies sweet
daf-fa-dil-lies sweet, these daf - fa-dil - lies sweet, daf-fa-dil - lies sweet
daf-fa-dil-lies sweet, let us a - bout these daf-fa-dil-lies sweet, daf-fa - dil - lies sweet
45

20. NOW MY LADS

* Charingo: charneco (corruption of Portuguese), a strong wine. ** Perry: cider made from pears.

EDITOR'S NOTES

1. General. This series is a thematic anthology of secular European madrigals and part-songs from the 16th and early 17th centuries. The settings are mainly for mixed four-part choir, but there are also some for three and five voices, and an occasional one for six. Five voices are strongly represented because this was an especially popular number in late 16th century madrigals. By and large, the items present relatively few vocal or harmonic difficulties for the fairly able choir, and where more than four parts are required, they are usually drawn from the upper voices (mainly the sopranos), with the tenor line hardly ever being split.

The term madrigal has been interpreted rather loosely. Besides the contrapuntal part-song, it relates to the frottola, ayre, chanson, lied and the villancico, whether courtly or folk (these all basically being harmonised melodies, often very simply set, and usually repeated for each stanza). More obviously, it encompasses the ballet (a short stanzaic setting in two sections with repeats and fa la las), and the canzonet (a lighter style madrigal, normally for a small number of voices). Rounds and catches have also been included because they were obviously an important component of a sing-song or a drinking party, certainly in 17th century England, and their choice of subject matter is very free-ranging. To help make madrigal concerts rather more of a party than a performance, at least two or three of the rounds in each volume have been selected as simple enough to be sung by an audience with or without a visual aid (see section 5 of these notes).

One of the most important features of this anthology is the arrangement by subjects, each volume being devoted to one of the prevalent topics in secular songs, for example, "The Animal Kingdom (vol. 1), "Love and Marriage" (vol. 2) and "Desirable Women" (vol. 3). This provides not only a new approach to madrigal anthologies but also, more importantly, a focus for the singers and, it is hoped, a comprehensible, appetising programme for the audience. Thus, it should be possible to provide a short concert entirely from one of these volumes, and two halves of a longer concert from any two.

Each volume contains at least twelve part-songs and, on average, half a dozen rounds. About one-third of the texts are in English, but an attempt has been made to provide a representative collection of Italian and French lyrics, and, to a lesser extent, of German and Spanish. The selection combines indispensable popular works with a fair mixture of relatively unfamiliar but attractive and singable pieces. Some thought has also been given to affording a balance between the lively and the reflective, the happy and the sad, for the sake of variety of mood and to help mirror the ups and downs of Renaissance life.

2. Editorial method. As with the Chester Latin Motet series, the Editor has endeavoured to make the volumes suitable for both performance and study. The madrigals are transposed, where necessary, into the most practical keys for ease of vocal range, are barred, fully underlaid in modernised spelling and punctuation, are provided with breathing marks, and have a simplified reduction as a rehearsal aid or as a basis for a continuo. Editorial tempi and dynamics have been supplied, but only in the reduction, leaving conductors free to supply their own according to their interpretation, vocal resources and the acoustics. The vocal range is given at the beginning of each piece, as also are translations for the non-English texts.

To help musicologists, the madrigals are transcribed from the most authoritative sources available. Original clefs, signatures and note values are given at the beginning and wherever they change during the course of a piece. Ligatures are indicated by slurs, editorial accidentals are placed above the stave, and the underlay is shown in italics when it expands a ditto sign, or in square brackets if entirely editorial. Where the original contains a *basso continuo*, it is included as the bass line of the reduction. Instrumental parts are transcribed within the relevant vocal lines as well as in the reduction. Finally, each volume contains brief notes on the scope of the edition, the composers, stylistic features of the part-songs, and the sources used, while editorial emendations and changes are given in footnotes within the text proper.

3. The themes and the lyrics. The widespread popularity of singing in the Renaissance is attested to by the vast numbers of song-books published throughout Europe with increasing frequency, especially in England, by the last two decades of the 16th century. By this time, secular compositions in print seriously rival sacred both in quantity and quality, and although they are mainly courtly, in the tradition of Petrarchan and pastoral lyrics, popular styles are also becoming more common, catering as they do for a more middle-class audience.

To be able to sing and to sight-read was a necessary attribute for a courtier. For example, Sir Thomas Hoby, in his translation of Castiglione's *Il Cortegiano* (1576), lists among the "chief conditions and qualities in a courtier" the ability to "sing well upon the book", "play upon the lute and sing to it with the ditty". Again in the section on "teaching to sing" in Thomas Morley's *Plain and Easy Introduction to Practical Music,* Philomathes, in a manner reminiscent of the poet Caedmon in Bede's account, feels ashamed of not being able to sing from a part-book when so requested by the lady of the house, and is subjected to the whispered comments of his fellow guests, who wonder how he could have been brought up in such ignorance. William Byrd strongly affirms the power of song: among the reasons he gives for learning to sing in the preface to his *Psalmes, Sonets and Songs* (1588) are that it is "delightful to Nature" and good for one's health; that it strengthens the chest and opens up the pipes; it is a good remedy for stuttering; and is a great aid to elocution and oratory. He adds that no musical instrument can ever equal the beauty of the voice and concludes:

> Since singing is so good a thing,
> I wish all men would learn to sing.

Though the notion of singing about singing may seem either odd or redundant, it is surprising how many texts there are on the subject, though they vary considerably in emphasis, as the present selection indicates. The most basic text, often encountered in rounds, is an exhortation to sing (with or without accompaniment) as an assertion of joy and fellowship (e.g.,

Sing with thy mouth, no. 9, ii, *Nun fanget an ein guts Liedlein*, no. 3); as an effective means of forgetting one's troubles, financial or otherwise (*Sing we now merrily*, no. 9, i); or as an appropriate accompaniment to drinking (*Now we are met*, no. 4). A natural extension of these functions is contained in the injunction to sing as a means of making hay while the sun shines, (*Sing we and chant it*, no. 7 – one of the numerous lyrics in the *carpe diem* tradition).

Many texts make play with the techniques of music, for example, the organisation of part-song into canon, fugue and homophony (e.g., in three parts in *Hey down a down*, no. 9, iv, and five parts in *Sing you now after me*, no. 9, iii). The gamut or six-note scale is particularly popular, used either in solmisation (sol-fa, with *do* being *ut*), or in the alphabetical sequence of G to E, both systems appearing in *Sol sol, GGABC*, no, 1 (a folk song in the Galician tradition), in which they form the basis of a happy but evasive song of a lovesick girl. Some songs reflect the Renaissance delight in *double entendre* in their treatment of the gamut. Thus, in *Vorria che tu cantass'* (no. 8), the exhortation to sing "fa mi la mi so la" could be construed as the request: "fami la mi sola", i.e., "do it for me alone". A similar link between singing and sexuality occurs in *Tutto lo dì* (no. 6), in which the frustrated lover is tired of singing to his aloof mistress's tune: she wants the detached romanticism of the love-song and the peal of hallowed bells; he would prefer the erotic music of sounding her cymbal.

Women figure prominently in relation to singing. *Chanter je veux* (no. 5) eulogizes the neoplatonic beauty of Catherine, about whom the poet needs to sing as if of the Virgin Mary, since she is not only the epitome of heavenly perfection but also the embodiment of divine music. A more cynical view is expressed in *Lieblich ich hörte singen* (no. 2), a text in the Lorelei tradition but rather more tongue in cheek. The message is clear: beware of the literal or metaphorical singing of the young women: they are sirens who will dash you on the rocks or cause you to drown in a sea of love.

Dancing has a prominence and a mystique in the Renaissance period which in some ways transcend the powers of song, for it was considered to be a reflection of the dance of the cosmos – a commonplace forming the basis of Sir John Davies' *Orchestra*:

> For your quick eyes, in wandring to and fro
> From East to West, on no one thing can glance,
> But if you mark it well, it seems to dance (stanza 34).

Thus, the sun is seen to dance a galliard (stanza 39), the moon a pavane (stanza 41), and the elements of earth, air, fire and water tread measures in their own distinctive way (stanzas 42ff.). Arbeau, one of the leading exponents of the dance in France, provides a long historical justification of the dance in his *Orchesographie* (1589) before describing most of the current popular dances in detail to his pupil Capriol; and Sir Thomas Hoby, in his list of attributes of the courtier mentioned above, includes the need to be able to "dance well without over-nimble footings or too busy tricks".

The references to dancing in the present selection are both general and particular. Like singing, the dance can be invoked as a means of pleasure and a liberation from care, preferably to be exercised in conjunction with drinking, as in *Sauter, danser* (no. 13) in which the undemanding but nevertheless coveted goal is to leap and skip, drink wine and count one's blessings (or, more specifically, one's money), while lazing in the sun. In no. 12, *Il ballerino*, the main aim is to set the music going in order to dance with one's beloved. A semi-figurative expression of exultation in the dance is provided by *Pouquoi-donc ne fringuerons-nous*? (no. 14), in which the defiant lover resolves to cavort with his mistress both in and out of bed, despite the public censure which is obviously born of envy. Among the more particular references to the dance, no. 11, *Chi la gagliarda*, deals with teaching the galliard, though it is clear that the experienced dancing-masters who encourage the fair ladies to learn it have something more than dancing in mind, as the refrain and the successive verses make increasingly clear. The English examples of dance-songs given here are all fairly specific. Two of them are types of masque dances, no. 10 being an elves' dance, and no. 15 a dance of satyrs. Of the remaining two, no. 16 is a combination of three country dances, and no. 17, *Strike it up, tabor*, features a Morris dance around the maypole. In most cases of a specified dance, it is likely to have actually been performed as well as sung.

Combined references to singing and dancing are very frequent in the period, since the two were natural sisters, especially in a pastoral setting, as in *Tanzen und Springen* (no. 18) and, more obviously, in *Sing we, dance we on the green* (no. 19). To add drinking to singing and dancing, as in *Now my lads* (no. 20), was to provide merriment that, temporarily at least, was invulnerable to the cares of the world. Not everyone, of course, viewed the twin arts with approval. In England, for example, the Puritans held both in suspicion as possible handmaidens of the devil. There was also a form of snobbery whereby court and town considered country song and dance to be, by and large, the activity of bumpkins.

4. The music. The first of the pieces about singing is a charming villancico from the famous Spanish manuscript collection, *Cancionero musical de Palacio* (Palacio Real, Madrid, MS 1335, f.45), where it is ascribed to Alonso, possibly Alonso de Pleja, about whom nothing is known but that he flourished around the beginning of the 16th century and composed both sacred and secular vocal music. He appears to have something of the rhythmic vitality and economy of Encina, though lacking the subtlety and intensity. The spry melody in duple time and the simple, occasionally awkward, harmony provide a good imitation of the girl's spontaneous vocalisation, sometimes following the exact scale of the solmisation, as in the cantus, bars 7ff.

Johannes Christoph Demantius was celebrated for his Passion, lieder and dances. He was born in Bohemia in 1567, studied at Wittenberg, and was employed as a cantor at Zittau and in Freiberg (in Saxony), where he died in 1643. His songs reflect the influence of Hassler, though they are rather more florid – a trait which is imitated in some degree by his pupil, Melchior Franck. The lied anthologised here, *Lieblich ich hörte singen*, was published in the Demantius collection, *Neue Teutsche Weltliche Lieder*, 1595 (complete set of copies in the Niedersächsische Staats-und Universitätsbibliothek, Göttingen). It has a smooth lyricism appropriate to the theme, expressive use of the two intertwining soprano voices to convey the lure of the sirens, and a flexible rhythm to accommodate the important verbal stresses. Widespread use is made of scale passages and there are two striking extended melismas for the upper voices in the first section to heighten the word-painting for the key syllables of "singen" and "jubilieren" – a technique which works almost equally well in the subsequent lines and strophes.

Hans Leo Hassler (1564–1612) was renowned both as a composer and as a keyboard player, holding diverse important posts as organist – for the influential merchant family of the Fuggers, the Imperial court, and for the Dresden court of Saxony. He studied in Venice under Andrea Gabrieli, and, as a result, the Venetian style, as well as the Italian style in general, influenced both his sacred and secular music. One of Hassler's many gifts is the ability to convey an exuberant joy in his music in a simple yet imaginative way, as exemplified in the two songs included here. Both derive from Hassler's best known collection of songs and dances, *Lustgarten Neuer Teutscher Gesang*, 1601 (complete set of copies in the Conservatoire Royal de Musique, Brussels), a work for which he also wrote the words. *Nun fanget an ein guts Leidlein*, for all its apparent simplicity, is remarkably varied, especially in its alternation of fugue and homophony and its different combinations of vocal lines, with the *tutti* sections reserved for the climaxes. The harmonies are a little more subtle than they initially appear, though after a beginning in the transposed Dorian mode, the piece moves mainly into G major and related keys.

Simon Ives (1600–62), a comparatively little known composer who lived in and around London, contributed several items to song collections, but most of his works are instrumental. The present song, from Hilton's *Catch That Catch Can*, 1652 (copy in British Library and in facsimile) is a brief extrovert piece with a strong melodic line and a lively dance rhythm. The harmonies are sparse and the parts widely separated as originally scored, so that it might be preferable to perform the top line an octave down.

The two pieces on singing by Lassus (biographical details in Volume 2) are in sharp contrast to one another, and again demonstrate his astounding versatility not only in musical styles but also in the range of lyrics selected. The five-part *Chanter je veux* derives from *Musica de' virtuosi della florida capella*, 1569, of which no complete set is extant in any one library, though Marsh's Library, Dublin, houses all but the Alto part, which is to be found, with the Bass, in the British Library. The setting is meditative, rich-textured, and in particular, very complex: for example, melodic lines are either smooth-flowing or highly syncopated; melismatic, as in the opening phrases for "chanter", or strictly monosyllabic, with many or no text repetitions. Harmonically, the mysticism of the Dorian mode pervades much of the piece, yet there is frequent modulation until the final cadence in the related major key. In its total effect, the madrigal has a devotional fervour more akin to the Lassus *offertoria* or *madrigali spirituali* than to a secular love-song. In completely different style is the canzone, *Tutto lo dì*, published in *Libro de villanelle, moresche, et altre canzoni*, Paris, 1581 (complete set of copies in the Biblioteca dell' Accademia Filarmonica, Verona), a collection in which the famous *Matona mia cara* also appeared (printed in Volume 3). The song, in Neapolitan style (aabcc), a swift-flowing businesslike, monosyllabic setting in this "dialogue of one", mainly in duple time but slipping into *sesquialtera* for the excited anticipation of fulfilment of a very frustrated desire (bars 33–6).

The simple balletto, *Sing we and chant it*, by Thomas Morley (biographical details in Volume 1) is indebted to Gastoldi (see below) not only in style but also greatly in content. It first appeared in Morley's *First Booke of Balletts*, 1595 (complete set of copies in British Library), and with the original Italian words in an Italian edition published the same year. This attractive piece in spry triple time and succinct phrases contains the usual lively flourish of fa la las, complete with the jaunty groups of four quavers leading off in dotted rhythm.

Antonio Scandello (1517–80), the next composer represented here, was a northern Italian who spent most of his life in Dresden, becoming Kapellmeister to the Electoral court in 1568. He published songs both in German (including his hen madrigal) and in Italian, in Neopolitan style, his *Vorria che tu cantass'* appearing in *El Primo Libro delle Canzoni Napolitane*, 1566 – the first entirely Italian collection of choral music published in Germany (complete set of copies in British Library). The song conveys Scandello's typical sense of humour and *bonhomie*. Like the Lassus *Tutto lo dì*, it begins in tuneful block harmony in duple time, but gradually introduces syncopation. This becomes rampant in the playful solfa scales, which, partly to observe the sexual pun (see preceding section), pay scant attention to following the contours of the actual scales represented, except fragmentarily in the tenor (bars 11–14), and even there inconsistently.

The section on singing closes with a group of rounds from the collections of Thomas Ravenscroft (biographical details in Volume 1), who either edited or composed a large number on this particular topic. Three of the rounds were published in Ravenscroft's *Pammelia*, 1609; the fourth, *Sing you now after me*, appeared in *Deuteromelia*, a companion collection published the same year (copies of both works in the British Library and in facsimile). The rounds provide a fair sampling of the variety to be found in Ravenscroft's collections, and range from three to eleven parts. The three-part *Hey down a down* is a canon at the fifth and the ninth, while the eleven-part round, *Sing we now merrily* – unfortunately the least effective melodically – has more than a touch of whimsy, since the last part comprises two whole bars of rests. The five-part *Sing you now after me* reserves the greatest amount of movement for the last line, with a little carillon on "ding dong". Its word-painting extends to conveying the notion of "five parts in unity" by a mainly chordal setting and by four of the parts ending at the unison or octave, though with a major third in the second part. The most tuneful of the set of rounds is *Sing with thy mouth*, which also has a lilting rhythmic grace.

The dancing section begins with a brief *Elves' dance* by John Bennet (c. 1570–c.1614), a minor but talented madrigal composer, who, in addition to publishing a volume of his own madrigals, contributed to the collections of others, including Morley's *Triumphs of Oriana* (1601). Bennet also collaborated with Ravenscroft in his psalter and provided several pieces for his *Briefe Discourse* (1614) including the present dance (copies in the British Library). Though unremarkable harmonically, the *Elves' Dance* is both delicate and intricate in rhythm, especially in the "trip and go" section with its fugal opening and quick syncopated figures. The time signature is ₵ (interpreted here as six-four time), but the triple time seems to yield to duple in bars 8–10, and has been so arranged editorially here, though without change of note values.

Baldassare Donato (c.1530–1603) spent most of his life in Venice, where he became a singer at St. Mark's and then, in 1590, *maestro di cappella* in succession to Zarlino, whose pupil he seems to have been. He published a volume of motets in the Venetian style and several of madrigals and villanellas. *Chi la galliarda* is one of his villanellas and first appeared in *Il Primo Libro di Canzon Villanesche alla Napolitana*, 1551 (transcribed here from the British Library copies of the 1558 edition). In form it is a lighthearted song set strophically, and, like the Neopolitan canzone, is divided into aabcc. Its duple rhythm becomes increasingly bold and jaunty, and ends in a galliard in which the fast triple time readily conveys the broad innuendo of the type of dances the masters really wish to teach.

Giovanni Giacomo Gastoldi, born near Milan c. 1550, spent his early musical life as a singer at the Gonzaga court in Mantua, becoming *maestro di cappella* in 1581, eventually having the young Monteverdi as a colleague. He remained there until 1609, moving then to a similar post at Milan Cathedral. He died in 1622. Although, as might be expected, Gastoldi composed a large quantity of sacred music, he is best known for his secular music, and, in particular, his five-part *balletti*, which proved of seminal importance, as already noted above. The present balletto derives from Gastoldi's three-part collection, *Balletti a tre voci*, 1594 (transcribed here from the British Library set of copies of the 1631 edition). As is usual with Gastoldi, the balletto has a subject heading, in this case, "the dancer", anxious to tread a measure with his lady. The style for the three-part balletto is even simpler than for the five-part: two brief repeated sections without even a fa la to extend the melodic line. Nevertheless, the piece has charm and delicacy, perfectly conveys the mood of both strophes, and makes a clever play between anticipation and fulfilment in the alternation of A major and minor (transposed here from G).

With *Sauter, danser* yet another example of Lassus' inventiveness is quickly apparent. It was published in *Thresor de musique d'Orlande de Lassus, contenant ses chansons*, 1576 (complete set of copies in Národní muzeum, Praha, Czechoslovakia). The chanson seems to leap and spring all over the page with a clash of underlying duple rhythm against the triple time in the beginning, a hocket style syncopation rampant in every part, and a wilful conflict of musical and verbal accent (somewhat reminiscent of the Lassus mass, *Octavi Toni*, where the same technique seems a weakness). There is also a continuous harmonic inventiveness which remains unpredictable until the final cadence, and there is hardly a cadential pause as the piece bustles on. Even for "compter écus au soleil", the music gives the impression of ceaseless energy rather than of an expected soporific indolence, the short busy figures prevailing to the end.

Pourquoi donc ne fringuerons-nous? by Pierre Passereau (biographical details in Volume 1), was first published in Attaignant, *Vingt et Sept Chansons Musicales à Quatre Parties*, 1533 (complete set of copies in the Bayerische Staatsbibliothek, Munich). It provides a similar type of liveliness to the preceding piece, though in the more formalised style of the madrigal, and its swiftness of movement is akin to that of Passereau's famous *Il est bel et bon* (published in Volume 1), especially in its sprightly use of *stretto* fugue. The assertiveness of the piece is reflected in the rising fourths and fifths of the opening and in the swift succession of syllables which almost give it the impression of a "patter song". Nevertheless, a strict sense of form prevails, with each section clearly delineated, and with roundedness provided by the aba form.

Ravenscroft's *Satyrs' dance* is a companion piece to the Bennet, both being found among a group of four dances in *A Briefe Discourse* (1614) mentioned above. Like the other dances, the *Satyrs' dance* is short and harmonically simple, relying heavily on thirds and tenths, especially in the opening. It is also supple and flexible in rhythm, with alternation of duple and triple time, and two sets of held chords both as punctuation marks and onomatopoeic exultant shouts of libidinous sun-worshippers. Yet another and more sophisticated Ravenscroft arrangement, this time from *Pammelia*, 1609 (copies in British Library and in facsimile), is *A round of three country dances in one*, in which three popular tunes, *The Cramp, Tomboy*, and *Robin Hood* are combined. The piece is more a quodlibet than a round, since the lines are separate melodies assigned to different parts, and even if the upper parts can be interchanged, the Bass or Ground remains independent and free. The integration of the melodies is masterly and worthy of comparison with Leonhard Paminger's *Christmas Motet*.

Strike it up, tabor is one of three songs on Morris-dancing by Thomas Weelkes (biographical details in Volume 1). It was published in his *Ayres or Phantasticke Spirites for three voices*, 1608 (set of copies in British Library), a collection notable for its varied and sometimes zany collection of lyrics. Conceived in a form very similar to the tobacco song, *Come, sirrah Jack, ho*, in the same collection (published in Volume 6), *Strike it up, tabor* has two short repeated sections, the first in triple time, the second in duple, and sets two strophes. Also in common with the tobacco song, it makes use of descending sequences and has (in the second section) a moving bass part in consecutive tenths with the cantus. A piece of great buoyancy and pace, *Strike it up, tabor* vividly portrays the springy vitality of a Maypole dance, and can easily be adapted as an accompaniment for one.

One of the most famous German Renaissance part-songs on the double pleasure of singing and dancing is Hassler's *Tanzen und Springen*, published in his *Lustgarten* mentioned above. The piece is in balletto style, which was very popular in Germany as well as in England at the time, and is clearly influenced by Gastoldi – indeed it could be construed as another variant of his *A lieta vita*, which Morley imitated in *Sing we and chant it*. It should be noted that although in some editions the second section is repeated to complete the aabb pattern, no repeat is indicated in the original.

Sing we, dance we, is a more extended piece on the same topic, being set as a full-scale pastoral madrigal, published in *First Set of Madrigals*, 1613 (complete set of copies in British Library). The composer, Francis Pilkington, was born probably in Lancashire around 1565, and spent most of his life in and around Chester, being employed for a time as a singer at the cathedral. Later, having entered holy orders in 1612, he held various curacies before becoming cathedral precentor in 1623 and rector of Aldford in 1631. He died in Chester in 1638. Pilkington published a volume of ayres and two of madrigals, which are usually refined and delicate almost to the point of preciosity. *Sing we, dance we* was published in Pilkington's *First Set of Madrigals*, 1613. It has an airy spaciousness, a great sense of continuity, and fine attunement to the rhythm and accentuation of the words. It marshals and varies its vocal resources with a skill similar to that of the large-scale works in the *Triumphs of Oriana*, and is particularly expressive in the bright sonorities of the two equal soprano parts.

The last composer in this anthology, Henry Lawes (1596–1662), was a brother of William Lawes, already represented in Volume 2 of this anthology. Henry became a member of the Chapel Royal in 1626 and was an ardent royalist. He was a master of the declamatory song and wrote for the theatre and for masques, providing the music for Milton's *Comus*. Like his brother, he contributed rounds to Hilton's *Catch that Catch Can*, 1652 (copy in British Library and in facsimile), including the present one, *Now my lads*, which, despite its uninspired words, is a roisteringly effective three-part round symbolically celebrating the pleasures of three kinds of drink and their furthering of the noble arts celebrated in this anthology.

5. Notes on programming. Since suggestions for performance have been given at length in the first two volumes, they are merely summarized here.

(i) The madrigals can be supplemented with solo songs on the same themes. Ideas for English songs can be gleaned from the revised edition of E. H. Fellowes, *English Madrigal Verse*, since it contains the lyrics for all the Elizabethan lute songs too. Other English sources include the pertinent volumes of *Musica Britannica* and the individual volumes of lute songs, also edited by Fellowes and subsequently revised.

(ii) Instrumental dances can be interspersed with the vocal items. A vast profusion exists for the European Renaissance. A particularly useful English collection for the later period is Andrew Sabol, *Four Hundred Songs and Dances from the Stuart Masque*, 1978.

(iii) Dances could be performed as part of the entertainment. Various text books are available as a guide, including the Dover Publications edition of Thinot Arbeau's *Orchesography*, 1967, and Mabel Dolmetsch, *Dances of England and France*, reprinted by the Da Capo press, 1976. In some cases, the dances in this volume are performable as such, notably *Strike it up, tabor*, which can serve as a maypole dance.

(iv) Readings can be interspersed with the music, for example, passages from the works referred to in section 3.

(v) A cyclorama or screen can be used on which to project slides of works of art corresponding to the music performed in theme, period and, where possible, provenance.

(vi) The audience should be encouraged to join in rounds and songs. Of the rounds in this collection, *Sing with thy mouth* and *Now my lads* should be well within the competence of an alert audience. The rounds selected can be projected on the screen used for the slides mentioned in (v) above.

チェスター社マドリガル楽譜シリーズ

このシリーズは、16世紀から17世紀初頭のヨーロッパのマドリガルと合唱曲を、目的別に集めたユニークなアルバムです。各巻はテーマ別に分けられ、第一巻は**動物**、第二巻は**愛と結婚**のシリーズになっています。各巻の解説にあるようにコンサートのプログラム作成にも便利です。

編成は混声四部合唱ですが、混声三部又は五部のものも若干含まれ、六部の曲もあります。

この曲集に入っているマドリガルは、最も有名でポピュラーなもの、魅力的で歌いやすいが余り知られていないもの等です。歌詞は、曲によってオリジナルの英語、イタリア語、フランス語、ドイツ語、及びスペイン語がついています。

チェスター社の**モテット楽譜シリーズ**と同様、この**マドリガル楽譜シリーズ**は演奏用、又は研究用に適するものとして作成されています。又、最も権威ある原典を資料にしていることは、音楽専門家にとって大変参考になります。